Samuel, Saul and David

(Types in 1 Samuel)

Charles Ozanne

I0159503

ISBN: 978-1-78364-466-7

The Open Bible Trust
Fordland Mount, Upper Basildon,
Reading, RG8 8LU, UK.

www.obt.org.uk

Samuel, Saul and David

(Types in 1 Samuel)

Contents

Page

Introduction

Introduction

There came a point in my reading of the Old Testament when I said to myself, "I know the historical facts pretty well by now. What is to be gained by reading them over and over again?"

It was at this point that I discovered *typology* – the amazing fact that the Old Testament is a vast picture gallery of New Testament truth. I knew about the types already, but had never before realized that almost every event and artifact has a hidden meaning pointing forward to the work of Christ and to God's long-term purposes for Israel and the world. It became clear to me that, so far, I had only scratched the surface of these books, and that a whole new vista of fascinating research lay before me.

Like John Bunyan's famous allegory, *Pilgrim's Progress*, the Old Testament shows the Christian reader what God is doing in his own life and in the world at large. But typology differs from allegory in that the Old Testament stories are true to fact, whereas an allegory is a fictitious story with a thinly disguised moral (or political) significance.

In the New Testament of few Old Testament types are explained for us by way of example. The fullest of these is Paul's explanation of Ishmael and Isaac in Galatians 4:21-31. The word "allegory" is used in this connection (v. 24, "which things being allegorized"), but the Greek word has a wider meaning than the English. There is no suggestion here that the original story is anything less than strictly true.

In 1 Corinthians 10 the events of the Exodus are given their counterparts in terms of Christian baptism and Christ's provision of spiritual food and drink. "These things", it is said, "occurred as examples (literally 'types') to keep us from setting our hearts on evil things as they did" (v. 6). Likewise in Hebrews 7 the brief description in Genesis of Melchizedek is shown to be a picture of Christ's eternal priesthood in heaven.

In modern terminology the word "type" is reserved for the Old Testament picture, while "antitype" is used of its New Testament counterpart. This is also true of the Bible though the words in question are used more generally. Thus it is said of Adam that he was "a pattern (type) of the One to come" Romans 5:14), and of baptism that is the "antitype of Noah's Flood (1 Peter 3:21).

My nascent interest in typology was given a tremendous boost by the discovery of Bishop Christopher Wordsworth's great work in eight volumes, *The Holy Bible in the Authorized Version with Notes and Introduction,* published in the 1870s and 80s. Because one volume was missing I was able to pick up all the others at a very reasonable price! This work is a veritable treasure-trove of typology – I have had occasion to quote from it several times in the course of the present booklet.

Bishop Wordsworth, a nephew of the poet, was a high churchman of the old school. He was the equal of any evangelical in his belief of the Bible, and the superior of most in respect of learning.

Samuel

Samuel

A child or promise

The picture is a familiar one which meets us in the first chapter of 1 Samuel. Elkanah had two wives, Peninnah and Hannah. Peninnah (meaning Pearl or Coral: pretty but hard and rough) had children, but Hannah (meaning Grace or Favour) was barren. The situation was similar with Sarah and Rachel, who were both goaded by their rivals. Hannah was taunted and teased by Peninnah before finally giving birth to the child of promise.

The meaning of the type is the same in each case. The loved but barren wife stands for the faithful Jewish remnant, her fertile but unsympathetic rival for the unbelieving Jewish synagogue, and the child of promise for true believers in Christ (so Galatians 4:21-31). In the highest sense the child of promise stands for Christ Himself, and there can be no question that Isaac Joseph and Samuel are all outstanding types of Christ.

The circumstances of Samuel's birth find a close parallel in the overall situation prevailing at the time of the nativity of Christ:

- a loving heavenly Father (represented by Elkanah),
- a hostile synagogue (corresponding to Peninnah), an ageing ceremonial (answering to Eli),
- a corrupt priesthood (exemplified by Hophni and Phinehas, compare Annas and Caiaphas),
- a faithful and prayerful remnant (typified by Hannah).

Under the tutelage of this well-intentioned but ineffectual ceremonial Samuel (like Jesus) was born and brought up. He submitted to it in humility and obedience, and there he learnt to worship the Lord (1 Samuel 1:28).

The word of the Lord was rare when Samuel was born, and visions were few (1 Samuel 3:1). Likewise at the birth of Jesus there had been no prophetic word for a very long time. There was nevertheless an air of expectancy that the time had come for God to act.

A temporary priesthood

Eli judged Israel for forty years – the same as the reign of Saul. Of the two surviving sons of Aaron the covenant of a lasting priesthood had been committed to the line of Eleazar because of the exceptional zeal of his son Phinehas when Israel joined in worshipping the Baal of Peor (Numbers 25). To this line belonged Zadok, David's faithful priest (2 Samuel 8:17; 15:24, cp. Ezekiel 44:15) and Azariah who served in Solomon's Temple (1 Chronicles 6:10).

Eli however belonged to the line of Ithamar (cp. 1 Chronicles 24:3) to whom no promise had been made of a lasting priesthood. This line held office in the days of Eli, Phinehas, Ahitub, Ahiah, Abimelech and Abiathar (1 Samuel 14:3; 22:20). These six possessed the high-priesthood in the days of the six men of Ezra's forebears who are omitted between Azariah and Meraioth in the genealogy of Ezra 7:1-5 (cp. 1 Chronicles 6:7-10).

Eli's caretaker priesthood interloped in the days of the Judges. It was purely transitional and temporary, and as such prefigures the temporary Aaronic priesthood as a whole. That priesthood, along with the old covenant of which it was a part, was ready to vanish away in the days of the apostles (Hebrews 8:13). Eli's temporary priesthood, together with Saul's temporary kingdom (for no promise of royalty had been made to the tribe of Benjamin), indicates the transitional character of 1 Samuel, prefiguring the transitory Jewish economy which still held sway in New Testament times.

Samuel's parents

Elkanah and Hannah were pious Jews who, like Joseph and Mary, journeyed regularly to worship the Lord at His prescribed sanctuary. On one such occasion Hannah, a woman of humble faith and believing prayer, received assurance from Eli (as Mary did from the angel) that she would bear a son. In due course the child was born, and Hannah in her profound gratitude promised to present him to the Lord at Shiloh, and there to leave him for ever. Likewise Joseph and Mary presented Jesus to the Lord at the time of their purification (Luke 2:22).

Hannah expressed her gratitude and joy in a song which bears a marked resemblance to the Magnificat of the Virgin Mary (1 Samuel 2, cp. Luke 1:46-55). Both songs begin with an outburst of joy and praise. Hannah says, "My heart rejoices in the Lord …. For I delight in your deliverance", and Mary, "My soul praises the Lord and my spirit rejoices in God my Saviour". Hannah goes on to praise the Lord for His holiness, firmness, and knowledge; and Mary speaks in a similar vein of the Lord's might, holiness and mercy. The Lord's knowledge is shown particularly in His abasement of the mighty and full, and in the exaltation of the feeble and hungry (2:5). So also Mary declares:

"He has brought down rulers from their
thrones
but lifted up the humble.
He has filled the hungry with good things
but has sent the rich away hungry."
(Luke 1:52-53)

Both hymns extol the Lord who exalts the lowly and brings down the proud and mighty. Hannah concludes her song with a stanza which clearly anticipates the final triumph of Christ:

"It is not by strength that one prevails;
    those who oppose the Lord will be shattered.
He will thunder against them from heaven;
    the Lord will judge the end of the earth.
He will give strength to his king
    and exalt the horn of his anointed."

Here for the first time the word Anointed (*meshiah*, Messiah) is used of the royal person by whom "the Lord will judge the ends of the earth".

In the "lending" of Samuel to the Lord and to the care of the high priest at Shiloh we may see a faint picture of what it meant to the Father to "send" His only begotten Son into the world. The sacrifice on the part of Elkanah and Hannah was small in comparison with that of the God and Father of our Lord Jesus Christ, but it must nevertheless have cost them a great deal to give up their only son to the care of the ageing high priest. Hannah was rewarded by the birth of three more sons and two daughters (2:21). These represent the expansion of the believing Jewish church after the birth of Christ. Elkanah, for his part, went back to Ha-Ramah (*the* High Place, 2:11), a picture of the position on high occupied by our Father in heaven. As for the child Samuel, he "continued to grow in stature and favour with the Lord and with men" (2:26). Practically the same words are used of the Lord Jesus in Luke 2:52 – "And Jesus grew in wisdom and stature, and in favour with God and men."

Eli's failure

In Eli's failure to check the scandalous behaviour of his priestly sons we may see how "weak and useless" was the old ceremonial (Hebrews 7:18-19). For the law can never, "by the same sacrifices repeated endlessly year after year, make perfect those who draw near to worship. Because it is impossible for the blood of bulls and goats to take away sins" (10:1, 4). Eli nevertheless would be judged for his failure to restrain his sons. A man of God, a prophet like John the Baptist, appears on the scene to predict the fate of Eli's house.

> "The time is coming when I will cut short your strength and the strength of your father's house, so that there will not be an old man in your family line and you will see distress in my dwelling. And what happens to your two sons, Hophni and Phinehas, will be a sign to you – they will both die on the same day." (2:31-34)

But he goes on to predict the rise of "a faithful priest, who will do according to what is in my (the Lord's) heart and mind. I (the Lord) will firmly establish his house, and he will minister before my anointed one (*meshihi*, my Messiah) always" (2:35).

This was fulfilled in Zadok (of the line of Eleazar and Phinehas) whom Solomon appointed priest in place of Abiathar, "fulfilling the word the Lord had spoken at Shiloh about the house of Eli" (1 Kings 2:27, 35). It will receive another fulfilment in "the sons of Zadok" who will keep charge of the sanctuary in the coming age, as the ministers of God's anointed one, Jesus Christ (Ezekiel 40:46; 44:15; 48:11).

The word of the Lord to Samuel

We come now to God's revealing Himself to Samuel as he lay in bed in the temple of the Lord (chapter 3). This occasion reminds us of our Lord's discussion with the Jewish rabbis in the Temple at Jerusalem when he was twelve years old. The message which Samuel received was in essence the same as that already pronounced by the man of God. But the boy Samuel was not puffed up (any more than Jesus) by the favour shown him or by the revelation granted to one so young. He did the daily work expected of him (3:15). He was meek and obedient as before, reverent and dutiful to Eli who was treated with contempt by his own sons. Therefore the Lord was with him increasingly, so that "all Israel from Dan to Beersheba recognised that Samuel was attested as a prophet of the Lord" (3:20). Jesus was also dutiful and obedient to Joseph and Mary (Luke 2:51).

The next chapter (4) signals the fulfilment of the previous prophecies insofar as Eli and his sons were concerned. The chapter spells total disaster (as indeed does 1 Samuel as a whole): the death of Eli, his two sons and daughter-in-law, the capture of the Ark by the Philistines, and the destruction of Shiloh. These events were a byword in disaster for centuries to come (Psalm 78:60-64; Jeremiah 7:12-14; 26:6, 9). Ichabod ("The glory has departed from Israel", 1 Samuel 4:21) is written across it. It was above all the superstitious trust in the Ark (corresponding to the Temple) which was Israel's and Eli's undoing. The same superstition marked the age of Jeremiah (7:4), the New Testament period, and every other age in which the outward form has taken the place of the inward reality.

These events foreshadow the end of the Jewish dispensation, the departure of God's presence from Israel, and the destruction of the Lord's sanctuary by the Romans. They also point forward to the coming of Christ (= Samuel), who is represented as already on the scene, brought up under the law, and awaiting His opportunity to take control of the situation.

Judgement on Dagon and the Philistines

Having captured the Ark of the Lord the Philistines took it first of all to Ashdod. There it was set beside the idol of Dagon in the temple of Dagon. In the morning, however, the idol had fallen on its face before the Ark. The following morning, not only had it fallen face downwards but had lost its most important members (its head and hands) in the process!

Wherever the Ark was taken it brought devastation and panic. At Ashdod and Gath the people were afflicted with painful sores, or tumours, as will be the worshippers of the Beast in a future day (Revelation 16:2, cp. Exodus 9:8-10). There was also a plague of rats and many of them died.

As in the book of Joshua the kings and gods of the Canaanites stand for principalities and powers in heavenly places. All these were defeated, crucified with Christ, at Calvary. He there disarmed the powers and authorities and made a public spectacle of them, triumphing over them by the cross (Colossians 2:15). It is the result of this triumph which is prefigured in 1 Samuel 5. The god Dagon, the visible symbol of the spiritual power in control of Ashdod, fell headlong and broke in pieces when placed alongside the Ark of the Lord. Likewise did the spiritual prince for which Dagon stood. The Philistines paid grudging honour to the God of Israel (1 Samuel 6:5), and so will every power in the universe acknowledge the supremacy of Christ (1 Corinthians 15:24, 25; 1 Peter 3:22; Philippians 2:9-11). This they will do with total conviction, not grudgingly like the Philistines.

The Ark returned to Israel

Seven months of this was all the Philistines could stand (1 Samuel 6:1), so they arranged for the Ark to be returned to Israel, and this is how they did it. They took a new cart and two cows that had recently given calf and had never been yoked.

These they hitched to the cart, but their calves they took from them and penned up in a separate enclosure. On the cart they put the Ark and beside it, in another box, the gold models of tumours and rats which they were sending as a guilt offering. They reasoned that if the cows, contrary to their maternal instinct, went up to Beth Shemesh on the Israelite side of the border, then the plagues were of the Lord. But if not, they had happened by chance.

The cows, contrary to nature, cut a straight course towards Beth Shemesh lowing plaintively all the way. The cart came to a stop in the field of one Joshua of Beth Shemesh just as he and the other inhabitants were harvesting their corn in the valley. When they looked up and saw the Ark approaching they rejoiced at the sight. Without delay they chopped up the wood of the cart and sacrificed the cows as a burnt offering to the Lord.

Such, in brief, is the story, but what does it mean? If I am not mistaken, we have here a quite remarkable type of the sacrificial death of the Lord Jesus Christ. The two cows represent Christ going to His death on the cross on Calvary as sin-offering for the world. They pulled behind them the wood on which they were sacrificed – just as Jesus carried His own cross, and Isaac carried the firewood on which he himself was to be laid (Genesis 22:6). It was a new cart because the cross of Calvary was a totally new event, nothing like it had happened before. And the cows had never before been yoked (like those of Numbers 19 and Deuteronomy 21) because Christ had never before submitted to the dictates of men.

The cows were lowing in anguish of soul, not in anticipation of their own fate, but in sorrowful yearning for their penned up calves back home. So Jesus wept over Jerusalem (Luke 19:41-44, cp. 13:34, 5). It was not His own fate which he lamented, but the fate of His children, the people of Israel, who were penned up in ignorance and gloom (Isaiah 42:7).

Every detail of this remarkable event carries significance. Why, for example, were there *two* cows and not one? It was not simply that the cart was heavy due to the living weight of the Divine presence (represented by the Ark) and the dead weight of human sin (represented by the guilt offering). There were two cows because Christ did not go alone to Calvary. He was accompanied by His heavenly Father (as Isaac was accompanied by Abraham). The two went together to be crucified for "God was in Christ reconciling the world to Himself" (2 Corinthians 5:19). The cows were sacrificed by the Jews but watched by the Gentiles (1 Samuel 6:16). So also was the crucifixion watched by Gentiles. The cows went straight to their appointed place, not deviating to the right or the left (6:12). Likewise Christ did not flinch from the path set before Him. He set His face like a flint knowing that His vindicator was near (Isaiah 50:7).

The cows came to a halt in the field of Joshua of Beth Shemesh, and the time was about Pentecost for they were harvesting their corn in the valley. The picture is an interesting one. The Ark, signifying the presence of God, is found resting in the field of Joshua, the Hebrew form of Jesus, and the time of year is Pentecost. The sacrifice of the cows, answering to the crucifixion, had just taken place. Without a doubt the scene prefigures the early chapters of Acts.

There was much rejoicing among the people. But there was also judgement. A large number was slain when they profanely looked into the Ark (6:19). In the Acts period also profanity was punished by sickness and death (1 Corinthians 11:30). As Paul said of the judgements in the wilderness, "These things happened to them as examples and were written down as warnings for us, on whom the fulfilment of the ages has come" (1 Corinthians 10:11).

From Beth Shemesh ("House of the Sun") the Ark was removed to Kiriath Jearim ("City of Woods") where it remained in the house of Abinadab until it was brought up by David to Jerusalem (2 Samuel 6:1-17; 1 Chronicles 13). Abinadab ("My Father is generous or noble") stands for all those who treasured the Lord's presence among them while the rest of the nation was in darkness and unbelief. Throughout this long period the Israelites did not enquire of the Lord (1 Chronicles

13:3). Nor in our day will they do so again until the presence of the Lord returns to Jerusalem.

Repentance and Victory

It was twenty long years before the people of Israel "mourned and sought after the Lord" – corresponding to the Acts period and, by implication, the many centuries of unbelief which continue to this day (1 Samuel 7:2). But they were not left without evidence of the Lord's saving power during this time. It was in fact during these twenty years that Samson was judge in Israel, as becomes clear when comparison is made with the book of Judges (see Keil on *Joshua, Judges and Ruth* p. 282). Samson opposed the Philistines single-handed while his countrymen look on in unbelief. He was a notable type of Christ in his miraculous feats of valour and victorious death. It may well have been his decisive conquest of the enemy, when he stretched out his arms in victory and death, that induced the Israelites to seek the Lord in repentance and faith. What clearer evidence could they ask for that God was still as powerful as ever and had not abandoned them in their humiliation and need?

The people as a whole put away their Baals and Ashtoreths and made up their minds to serve the Lord alone. They were now "afraid because of the Philistines" (7:7), in contrast with their misplaced elation prior to their defeat at Aphek (4:5). They now called upon Samuel to pray for their deliverance. Samuel therefore "cried out to the Lord on Israel's behalf, and the Lord answered him" (7:9).

In the ensuing battle "the Lord thundered with loud thunder against the Philistines" (7:10) – as he had promised to do when the time should come to "judge the ends of the earth" (2:10). We have here a foretaste of this end-time judgement. The Philistines were defeated with a great slaughter and "did not invade Israelite territory again" (7:13). Not only did Israel get back the cities they had lost to the Philistines, but "there was peace between Israel and the Amorites" – that is the Canaanites in general (7:14).

Samuel set up a stone to commemorate the occasion. He called it Eben-ezer, Stone of Help, saying, "Thus far has the Lord helped us" (7:12). Samuel judged Israel for the rest of his life. Each year he did the circuit of Bethel, Gilgal and Mizpah, and then returned to the Height (ha-Ramah) where were his permanent abode and judicial seat. This would suggest that Christ will not remain on earth throughout the age to come, but will visit it from time to time.

Conclusion

The first seven chapters of 1 Samuel present in microcosm the message of 1 Samuel as a whole. Samuel's nativity and humble deportment under Eli's tutelage clearly prefigure the birth and submissive childhood of the Lord Jesus, in obedience to His parents and the religion of His forefathers. Israel's humiliation at Aphek, the capture of the Ark, and the departure of God's glory from the land (Ichabod, No-glory) prefigure the destruction of the city and Temple by the Romans and the end of the Jewish dispensation.

There is a long interval during which Israel was unable to enquire of the Lord. But at the end of this period the tables were turned on the Philistines in response to Israel's repentance and supplication. And so it will be in the future when God intervenes on Israel's behalf "with thunder and earthquake and a great noise, with windstorm and tempest and flames of a devouring fire" (Isaiah 29:6). After this victory Samuel is recognised as Judge and a period of national peace ensues.

David's fortunes under Saul, before he is recognised as King of Israel, follow a similar pattern to those of Samuel. The words of the Lord Jesus on the Damascus road, "Saul, Saul, why do you persecute Me?" are the key to the underlying meaning of these chapters. We turn therefore to our next character, Saul, the Lord's anointed and David's persecutor.

Saul

Saul

The subject of our last chapter was Samuel – a notable type of Christ in his miraculous birth, dedicated upbringing, prophetic ministry and final triumph. In the rest of 1 Samuel he plays a less important part. As first in the roll-call of prophets (for as such he is represented in Acts 3:24; 13:20 and Hebrews 11:32) Samuel stands for the voice of prophecy, the directing, teaching, reproving, appealing, promising and condemning word of Almighty God.

The part of Christ, chosen from obscurity and after many trials established as king, is taken by David. Saul the interloper stands for Israel under the dispensation of law. His kingdom, concerning which no promise had been made in earlier times, was strictly parenthetical and preparatory – until the one should come to whom the promise had been made (cp. Galatians 3:19).

The law was "added because of transgressions", just as Saul was chosen to be king as a result of

Israel having rejected the Lord (1 Samuel 8:7; 10:19; 12:17). The beginning of the dispensation of law was fair and promising like the reign of Saul, and marked by extraordinary tokens of God's favour and protection. It was also marked by promises and threats of judgement if the people did not obey the Lord, as was the reign of Saul (12:12-25). Like Saul, however, it degenerated into the sullen, suspicious, inward-looking system which was to persecute and kill the Lord and His disciples. As such, it was rejected by God, and was finally overrun by heathen armies as Saul was by the Philistines. Hence the first book of Samuel ends at the point foreshadowed in 1 Samuel 4 – Israel in confusion, the glory departed, and the Philistines in control.

Among the family of Saul, however, there was one man whose love for and loyalty to David knew no bounds. This man was Jonathan, meaning "the Lord has given", whose love for David is described as "wonderful, more wonderful than that of women" (2 Samuel 1:26). He is a type of those Hebrew Christians who counted their Jewish ancestry as nothing compared to the surpassing

greatness of knowing Christ Jesus their Lord
(Philippians 3:8).

We will consider first the character of Saul. It will
not be possible to look at everything that is said of
him – a method which would lead to too extensive
a treatment. By selecting certain passages I will
seek to uncover his typical and prophetic
significance.

The choice of Saul

Saul is an excellent example of the principle that
the spiritual is preceded by the natural, for "the
spiritual did not come first, but the natural, and
after that the spiritual" (1 Corinthians 15:46). Saul
was one of nature's finest sons: "an impressive
young man without equal among the Israelites – a
head taller than any of the others" (1 Samuel 9:2;
10:23). There was none like him among all the
people of Israel. He was just the sort of king which
the natural man desired, one distinguished by
physical strength, natural beauty, and bodily
stature. They had asked for a king, and they got

what they asked for! Such is the meaning of Saul – Sha'ul, asked for.

Dispensationally he stands for Israel under the covenant of law, this being both the consequence of the people's sin and the occasion for greater sinfulness. "For sin, seizing the opportunity afforded by the commandment, deceived me, and through the commandment put me to death," says Paul (Romans 7:11). The people were warned that their king would prove a hard taskmaster (1 Samuel 8:10-18), and such indeed he became as did the law in conjunction with human sinfulness. "You yourselves will become his slaves," Samuel had said (8:17); and it is the testimony of Paul that the law had made slaves of them all. Nevertheless, the law itself was holy, just and good, and this is shown in Saul's humble, unassuming behaviour at the outset of his reign.

More than anyone else, the counterpart of King Saul is Saul of Tarsus, Pharisee, fanatic and persecutor. Just as Saul of Tarsus hounded Christians to their death, so King Saul relentlessly hunted David with a view to killing him. As such he was typical of Pharisaic Judaism as a whole seeking to stamp out the Christian church in its infancy. But Paul speaks of a time when once he was alive apart from the law (Romans 7:9). He refers, one assumes, to his childhood before the law with its binding regulations had got a stranglehold on his mind and actions. This state of youthful innocence is reflected in 1 Samuel 9 when Saul is seen going about his father's business still unaware of the tremendous yoke about to be foisted on him. It was the same with Israel in the early days of their history, before they were yoked with the law and enslaved by its commandments.

Saul's success and failure

Saul's first encounter was with Nahash the Ammonite who had encamped against Jabesh-gilead on the east of Jordan (1 Samuel 11). Nahash means "serpent", the best known symbol of the Devil, while the settlers on the other side of Jordan stand for Old Testament Israel as in the book of Joshua. The men of Jabesh thought they could come to terms with Nahash, agreeing only to be subject to him. But Nahash as a condition of peace, demanded not only their subjection but also the right eye of each and every one. Without their right eyes they would have been useless in battle. Such is the cost of making an alliance with the devil.

On this occasion, however, a great salvation (*teshu'ah*, vs. 9, 13) was accomplished over the old serpent by the hand of Saul and Samuel. Saul ascribes the victory entirely to the Lord (v. 13). In this we may see what could be accomplished under the old covenant when there was complete obedience to the Lord as revealed to His prophet. Nahash was completely routed so that not two of his followers were left together. As for Saul, "all the people went to Gilgal and confirmed Saul as king in the presence of the Lord" (v. 15).

Saul excelled himself on this occasion, but it was not long before his inherent weakness and failure began to show itself. At the same time his son Jonathan begins to emerge as God's faithful warrior (cp. 13:3). Saul had by then drifted so far from the Lord that he refers to his own people as

"Hebrews" (13:3) – the name used by the Philistines and other Gentiles (4:6; 13:19; 14:11; 29:3). The name comes up again in verse 7 where we read that "some Hebrews", because of the great distress in the land, "even crossed the Jordan to the land of Gad and Gilead". They had, as it were gone back on their circumcision at Gilgal (where the reproach of Egypt had been rolled away, Joshua 8), and returned to wandering in the wilderness.

Saul, it is true, was still at Gilgal, but his heart was not true to the Lord. Because Samuel did not come and his men were beginning to scatter, Saul took it upon himself, in defiance of the Lord's command, to make the intended sacrifice himself. He thought he would be all right since he had fulfilled the required ceremonial. Like the Pharisees he trusted in the externals of religion rather than in true faith obedience. Worse still, he usurped the place reserved for Christ, for He alone is both King and Priest.

For this disobedience Saul was told that his kingdom would not continue. When he was obedient he had gone out against the Ammonites in three companies (11:11); now the Philistines came against him in three companies (13:17-18). The end of the chapter reveals the straits the people were now in – they had not even a weapon for self-defence. The Philistines stand for the realm of the uncircumcised both outside and within. Saul never succeeded in overcoming either the enemy on his doorstep or the uncircumcision of his own heart. Failing to overcome, he was finally slain by the resurgent Philistines. Likewise the Jewish nation was initially overrun and finally destroyed by the uncircumcised Romans.

Saul's sad decline

Saul's weakness for legalistic observances, in preference to heart-obedience, is seen again in the next chapter (14). It was Jonathan, not Saul, who turned the tables on the Philistines in a personal enterprise of great daring. At this time Saul, the caretaker king, along with Ichabod's nephew, the caretaker high priest, was taking his ease under the pomegranate tree in Migron, quite unaware of what Jonathan was doing. While Saul was content with the ordinances of religion and the company of its priestly representatives, it was Jonathan who was actively trusting the Lord for victory over the Philistines.

Jonathan's irrepressible faith may be seen in the things which he said: "Nothing can hinder the Lord from saving, whether by many or by few" (v. 6); "that will be our sign that the Lord has given them into our hands" (v. 10); "Climb up after me; the Lord has given them into the hand of Israel" (v. 12). With the help of his armour-bearer he slew about twenty men, an act of believing courage which the Lord confirmed by causing the earth to shake and by sending panic into the whole Philistine army.

The Philistines were in total disarray, even killing one another in their panic and confusion. If ever an opportunity existed to break their power once and for all, now was the time. But instead of imitating his son's obedience and gaining total victory over the Philistines in the same spirit of daring faith, Saul interposed with a legalistic command which all but wrecked this heaven-sent opportunity. He cut the supply of divine grace (the honey of God's promises, Psalm 119:103) by the foolish command, "Cursed be any man who eats food before even comes, before I have avenged myself on my enemies!" (v. 24). He is confident that he himself is equal to the task, forgetful that vengeance belongs to the Lord.

Being ignorant of his father's oath, Jonathan did not hesitate to eat some of the honey which was in plentiful supply in the woods they had entered. When he tasted the honey his eyes became bright. But all the rest of Saul's army, not daring to disobey the king, were faint and exhausted, so much so that when the evening finally came, they fell on the plundered sheep and calves and devoured them raw with the blood still in them, contrary to the law.

Saul was still pursuing the Philistines by night. But when, at the priest's suggestion, he enquired of the Lord, God did not answer him. Concluding from this that a sin had been committed, he uttered another foolish oath, "As surely as the Lord who rescues Israel lives, even if it lies with my son Jonathan, he must die" (v. 39).

So he cast the lot between himself and Jonathan on the one side and all Israel on the other, and he and Jonathan were taken. He then called on it to decide between himself and Jonathan, and Jonathan was taken. Saul was quite prepared to kill his own son, even though Jonathan had acted in ignorance of his command. But this was too much for his men. They intervened on Jonathan's behalf and narrowly rescued him. And Saul was humiliated in the presence of his own subjects.

Saul's order not to eat anything before sundown was the cause of the people's sinning, his own humiliation, and very nearly led to the execution of his own son. Like Achan, he had troubled Israel (14:29), not in this instance by appropriating something which had been devoted to destruction (as in the next chapter), but by forbidding the people to enjoy what the Lord had provided. His fault was the same as that of Pharisaic Judaism, "Do not handle! Do not taste! Do not touch!" (Colossians 2:20-23). As a result of his failure the

Philistines were never defeated in his lifetime. Under Samuel's leadership "the Philistines were subdued and did not invade Israelite territory again" (7:13). But "all the days of Saul there was bitter war with the Philistines" (14:52).

Saul's downfall confirmed

Saul was told by the Lord through Samuel to punish the Amelekites for their perpetual hostility to Israel from the time of the Exodus onwards (cp. Exodus 17:8-16). Saul's instructions were perfectly clear, "Now go, attack the Amelekites and totally destroy everything that belongs to them. Do not spare them; put to death men and women, children and infants, cattle and sheep, camels and donkeys" (15:3).

Saul, however, at the instigation of his army, "spared Agag (the king of the Amelekites) and the best of the sheep and cattle – everything that was good". And it is added by way of explanation, "These they were unwilling to destroy completely, but everything that was despised and weak they totally destroyed" (15:9).

Saul is nevertheless adamant when confronted by Samuel that he had carried out the Lord's instructions to the letter (vs. 13, 20), insisting that the sheep and cattle were spared "in order to sacrifice to the Lord your God at Gilgal" (v. 21). Saul here speaks of "your (Samuel's) God", as if he were doing Samuel a favour! This draws from Samuel a prophetic utterance of far-reaching import:

> "Does the Lord delight in burn offerings and sacrifices as much as in obedience to the voice of the Lord? To obey is better than sacrifice, and to heed is better than the fat of rams. For rebellion is like the sin of divination, and arrogance like the evil of idolatry. Because you have rejected the word of the Lord, he has rejected you as king." (15:22-23)

Saul's sin was twofold: covetousness and a fear of the people. He coveted the best of the sheep and cattle and he was afraid of incurring the army's displeasure by acting contrary to their wishes, even though the Lord had commanded that everything should be destroyed. He does finally confess, "I was afraid of the people and so I gave into them" (v. 24). How closely Saul and the people are associated in the statement, "But Saul and the army (literally "people") spared Agag and the best of the sheep and cattle"! As Adam laid the blame on Eve, so Saul lays the blame on the people – "The soldiers ("people") brought them from the Amalekites; *they* spared the best of the sheep and cattle" (v. 15).

These were also the faults of the scribes and Pharisees whom Saul foreshadows. The Pharisees were covetous (Luke 16:14); they also "were afraid of the people" (Luke 20:19; 22:2; Acts 5:26). In contrast Paul declares, "Am I now trying to win the approval of men, or of God? Or am I trying to please men? If I were still trying to please men, I would not be a servant of Christ" (Galatians 1:10; 1 Thessalonians 2:4).

Like Achan, Saul kept for himself that which had been devoted to destruction (v. 21). He boasted that he had obeyed the Lord fully (vs. 13, 20). So pleased was he with his own achievement that "he set up a monument in his own honour" at Carmel (v. 12). Likewise the Pharisees were quick to profess their own righteousness when there was no real heart-obedience at all. Saul should have heeded the exhortation in Exodus 23:2, "Do not follow the crowd in doing wrong".

A final word

It is all too easy to point the finger at Saul for his weakness and disobedience, and to feel complacently that we would never act in such a way. But Saul's life is given for our instruction and warning. His faults are precisely the ones which we ourselves are most likely to fall into. We are all extremely prone to go our own way, to trust in our own strength, to fear for our fragile reputation, to follow the crowd, to trust in formal acts of worship etc. There is therefore no room for complacency. We are all Sauls at heart apart from the grace of God.

> So if you think you are standing firm, be careful that you don't fall! (1 Corinthians 10:12)

Work out your salvation with fear and trembling, for it is God who works in you to will and to act according to his good pleasure. (Philippians 2:12-13)

David

David

The Son of Jesse

From 1 Samuel 16 primacy is given to the story of David, the man after God's heart, the most notable type of Christ in the Old Testament. As for Saul, in his persecution of the true heir, he becomes more and more like his deluded namesake, Saul of Tarsus, prior to his conversion. Saul of Tarsus, the embodiment of Pharisaic Judaism, made it his aim to stamp out the infant church of Christ. So King Saul did his worst to destroy the one whom he knew was destined to succeed him as king. In our reading of this history we shall do well to remember the words of Bishop Wordsworth:

> "The histories of Saul and David acquire a new interest for us Christians, when we see in the former a picture of those sins for which the literal Israel has been cast off by God, and in the latter an image of those graces, by which alone we can hope to be partakers of the kingdom of Christ."

The choice of David

In 1 Samuel 16 we learn how David, the youngest and least significant of Jesse's eight sons, was anointed by Samuel, and then how his skilful playing soothed the troubled spirit of the deserted king. Doubtless there were many scions of the house of David more noble or noteworthy than the infant son of the virgin Mary. Yet, Like David, it was He who was anointed with the oil of gladness above his fellows (Psalm 45:7; Hebrews 1:9). He was "the Christ of God, the Chosen One" (Luke 23:35), "the living Stone – rejected by men but in God's sight chosen and precious to Him" (1 Peter 2:4).

David was young and insignificant compared with his tall and handsome brothers. Likewise, "God chose the weak things of the world to shame the strong. He chose the lowly things of this world and the despised things – and the things that are not – to nullify the things that are, so that no-one may boast before Him" (1 Corinthians 1:27-29).

Saul by this time was possessed by an evil spirit. He was melancholy, gloomy, irritable, violent, envious and suspicious. David played on the harp and Saul was refreshed. So Jesus Christ spoke comforting words to the Israel of His day; He laid His hand on the sick and cast out devils. Many were refreshed, but the nation as a whole grew worse rather than better. It was as if He played the flute for them, but they would not dance (Luke 7:32).

Despite his success in soothing the king, David was still unknown to Saul after killing Goliath (17:55-58). Likewise Jesus was not known to the world (John 1:10), even after He had moved among them, healing the sick and delivering them from the power of Satan. Saul asked, "Whose son is that young man?" The Jews still do not know whose son Christ is, and their leaders (the Pharisees) cannot tell them. See Matthew 22:41-45 and John 8:19.

David and Goliath

We pass now to the story of David and Goliath. Generations have been inspired by this account of youthful trust and heroism. But what, we wonder, is its deeper typical meaning?

We notice first of all that Goliath is called "*ish habbenaim*, the man between, *viz* the two armies. He poses as mediator, but unlike Christ he comes to enslave the people of God by killing their representative. In all aspects he stands for the Devil. Twice daily for forty days he came forward with his terrifying challenge. It was also for forty days that Christ was tempted by the Devil. But the number forty stands for the whole Jewish dispensation throughout which it was the Devil's constant ambition to destroy the people of God, and especially the seed royal from which the Messiah would eventually spring. We see him here reviling, defying, and ridiculing the army of Israel as he still does believers in Christ, and as he will do again the people of Israel by means of his chosen representative, the Antichrist.

In this tense situation David appeared on the scene, sent by his father with loaves and cheeses for the sustenance of his brothers and their commanding officers. He came in all innocence, seeking only the welfare of his brothers according to the flesh. We think of the young Joseph sent by his father Jacob on a similar errand and being sold into slavery for his pains. All of them dismissed with contempt any thought of David himself engaging the Philistine in single-handed combat. He was only a callow youth, they argued, a presumptuous boy totally unfit for such an enterprise. In much the same way Christ was rejected by His own brothers while He was still with them (John 7:5). His countrymen took offence at Him because His 'father' was only a carpenter, and His brothers and sisters well known to them. They could not credit that someone so familiar to them could be the Christ of God. So also the Pharisees rejected Him because He was not a Pharisee like themselves, trained in the subtleties of the Law. Like Saul they would have harnessed Him with their own armoury of legal regulations. Christ, however, cut through the legal jungle and overcame the Devil armed only with the word of God and total obedience to the will of God.

David went to meet the Philistine with his shepherd's staff in his hand, his sling and five smooth stones from the brook. The five stones stand for the books of the Law. He took all five, but like Christ confronting the Devil he needed only one. That stone struck Goliath in the forehead, the seat of impious effrontery. As David slew Goliath with a single stone, so Christ overcame the Devil with three darts from the book of Deuteronomy. And David, having stunned him, cut off the giant's head with the Philistine's own sword. The Philistine was slain with his own instrument of death like Haman crucified on the gallows intended for Mordecai. So Christ, by death, destroyed him that had the power of death – the Devil (Hebrews 2:14). To outward appearance it was Christ who was killed, but in reality it was the Devil, while Christ rose from the dead to a fuller and more glorious life.

David took Goliath's head and brought it to Jerusalem. The city, still in Jebusite hands, was thus given a pledge of its future deliverance by David's son and heir. When that takes place their true King will reign in Mount Zion, and the Devil, now totally defeated, will be bound for a thousand years.

Jonathan

Bishop Wordsworth prefaces his comments on 1 Samuel 18 with the following words:

> "Jonathan, the son, is contrasted with Saul, the father (see above, 14:1). Saul is more and more estranged from David. Jonathan is more and more attached to him. Jonathan prefigures the faithful Israel of God, who hailed the advent of the true David and rejoiced in his triumphs: Saul typified the envious and malignant Scribe and Pharisee who desired to destroy him. Jonathan represents those loving souls who were born and lived under the Law …"

This threefold tug-of-war is played out at length in the rest of 1 Samuel.

We have already seen how Jonathan, single-handed, accomplished a rout of the Philistines in chapter 14. Not only were the Philistines defeated as a result of Jonathan's faith obedience, but the Israelites themselves were spiritually revived. Those who had joined forces with the Philistines (the worldly and disillusioned) now returned to Saul and Jonathan. Likewise those who had hidden themselves in the hill country of Ephraim (the lonely and defeated) took up arms and joined the battle (14:21-22).

Jonathan's eyes were made bright when he ate of the honey dripping in the forest. One is reminded of Psalm 19:8, 10, "The commands of the Lord are radiant, giving light to the eyes…They are sweeter than honey, than honey from the comb". Jonathan stands for those Jewish believers who used the word of God correctly for their own spiritual enlightenment, whereas Saul, the forerunner of the scribes and Pharisees, neither took of the honey himself nor allowed anyone else to do so insofar as it was in his power to prevent them.

In chapter 18 we find Jonathan stripping himself of every insignia of office and rank and giving them to David. "Jonathan took off the robe he was wearing and gave it to David, along with his tunic: and even his sword his bow and his belt" (18:4). Though heir presumptive to the throne he was happy to relinquish his rights in his love for David. He prefigures all those who, like the apostle Paul, considered their Jewish privileges as rubbish compared to the surpassing greatness of knowing Christ Jesus their Lord (Philippians 3:7-11).

In chapter 20 we reach the final separation between David and Saul, with Jonathan acting as intermediary. David suspecting that Saul was planning to kill him, had absented himself from the new moon festival. Saul predictably flew into a rage when he heard from Jonathan the trumped-up excuse for David's absence, and even tried to kill his own son. The next day Jonathan went out into the field where David was hiding and warned him of his father's intentions by means of the pre-arranged sign. They then kissed each other and departed, David as a fugitive from the king's wrath and Jonathan back to the city where he belonged.

In this incident is prefigured the scattering of the disciples as a result of the persecution following the martyrdom of Stephen – that is "all except the apostles" (Acts 8:2-4; 11:19). The leading persecutor was none other than Saul of Tarsus (8:3). Just as Saul the king hunted David like a wild animal in his mad determination to kill his most loyal subject, so Saul of Tarsus persecuted the true David with a blind and fanatical fury. It was Christ Himself whom Saul persecuted in the persons of His humble followers (Acts 9:4). Saul persecuting David corresponds to Saul persecuting Christ, but Saul of Tarsus was only the representative of the Jewish leaders who authorised his activities.

Jonathan, while staying with his father, remained loyal to David. And here we think of the twelve remaining at Jerusalem at great risk to themselves because Jerusalem was still the centre of God's Kingdom and Church. Wordsworth truly comments:

"Jonathan, Saul's son was a figure of all those faithful Israelites …. Whose hearts were knit to Christ, and who made a solemn covenant with Him, even at the time when He was rejected and persecuted by the Jewish Saul; and looked forward in faith to the time when the kingdom of the true David would be established, and His foes made His footstool, and His enemies be cut off before His face, and who prayed to Him to show mercy to themselves personally in their own lifetime, and to their posterity after their death, for evermore (see 20:14, 15), and who incurred danger, scorn, and death from their own parents and relatives, for the sake of Christ:" (v. 33)

Jonathan said to David, "You shall be king over Israel, and I will be second to you. Even my father Saul knows this" (23:17). And so it is promised by Christ to the faithful Israelite, "To him who overcomes, I will give the right to sit with me on my throne, just as I overcame and sat down with my Father on His throne" (Revelation 3:21).

David eats the consecrated bread

In 1 Samuel 21 we read how David availed himself of the Bread of the Presence which it was not lawful for any but the priests to eat. The priest Abimilech gave it to him out of loyalty to the king who had sent David (or so David claimed) on a secret mission. He did so in all innocence not knowing how things stood between David and Saul. By eating the Bread of the Presence David showed himself superior to the ceremonial law which was fulfilled in Christ and applied only until the time of the new order (Hebrews 9:10). David therefore foreshadowed Christ, the one who fulfilled and superseded the Law (see Mark 2:23-28).

Unfortunately for Abimilech there was a traitor in his midst, namely Doeg the Edomite. Doeg saw what happened, reported it to Saul, and then returned with the king's authority to kill the priests at Nob, 85 persons that wore the linen ephod. Doeg is described as "Saul's head shepherd" (21:7)! But a truer description of him is to be found in Psalm 52:

"Why do you boats of evil, you mighty man?
Why do you boast all day long?
You are a disgrace in the eyes of God?
Your tongue plots destruction:
It is like a sharpened razor,
You who practice deceit

…

Here now is the man
Who did not make God his stronghold
But trusted in his great wealth
And grew strong by destroying others!"

Doeg is participial in form, meaning the one who is anxious (1 Samuel 9:5; 10:2) or afraid (Jeremiah 38:19; 42:16; Isaiah 57:11). The actual word *doeg* occurs in Jeremiah 38:19 where Zedekiah says "I am afraid of the Jews who have gone over to the Babylonians". Doeg stands for the Jews generally (and Judas in particular) who were *anxious* or *afraid* for their privileges and traditions. The Jewish leaders were afraid of the people because they held Jesus to be a prophet (Matthew 21:46) and followed the apostles (Acts 5:26). Both Saul and Doeg were afraid of anyone who posed a threat to their privileged position by siding with David.

It should be noted that Abiathar, who was later high priest, was also present on this occasion. In fact he alone escaped to tell the tale (22:20; 23:6). It is not therefore incorrect to say (allowing for normal conventions of language) that David ate the consecrated bread "in the days of (or "in the place relating to") Abiathar the high priest" (Mark 2:26). Abiathar belonged to the caretaker priesthood descended from Eli and Ithamar. He remained in office throughout David's reign answering to the fact the temporary Aaronic priesthood will not be replaced until the reign of Christ in glory foreshadowed by Solomon.

David the fugitive

David was not a fugitive from Saul, hiding in caves and desert places. He was accompanied by a motley crew of malcontents and debtors, united in only one thing, their loyalty to David. They are a type of the early church, a motley crowd indeed, but united in their loyalty to the rejected Christ and unmovable in their confidence that one day He would be recognized as King and Lord of all. In the meantime they are willing to suffer every kind of scorn and deprivation that they might be considered worthy to reign with Him in His kingdom (2 Timothy 2:12; Revelation 3:21; Romans 8:17).

David made a surprise attack on the Philistines who were busy robbing the threshing floors of Keilah. David "saved the people of Keilah" (1 Samuel 23:5), but they were still prepared to deliver him into the hands of Saul (v. 12). Likewise the cities in which Christ did most of His mighty works refused to repent, and drew from the Lord His strongest condemnation (Matthew 11:20-24). It was however David who had the ear of the Lord and was directed by his word (23:1-12), while the Lord had departed from Saul (16:14; 18:12).

Saul tried repeatedly to kill David, but David never faltered in his loyalty or retaliated in any way. Even when he had Saul completely in his power, he refused to do more than cut off a piece of his garment and even that was more than his conscience could bear! (24:3-5). By his loyalty and forbearance David heaped coals of fire – of shame and remorse – on Saul's head (Romans 12:20). The Jews tried to kill the Lord and His disciples, but the latter did not return evil for evil, nor insult for insult, but rather blessing (1 Peter 3:9). They remembered their Lord's command, "Love your enemies and pray for those who persecute you" (Matthew 5:44; Luke 6:27-28).

Nabal the rich fool

If ever there was a rich fool it was Nabal (chapter 25). He had great possessions but would not share them with a living soul. David had done him a great service in protecting his shearers and their belongings during the season of shearing (25:15, 16, 21). But Nabal professed to have no knowledge of David except that he was a renegade who had broken faith with his master! David in his anger was fully prepared to teach Nabal a well-earned lesson, even to the point of destroying every male in his household. From this course of action he was only just restrained by the humble entreaties and generosity of Nabal's wife Abigail. Only ten days later Nabal was struck down by the Lord, and Abigail, who had impressed herself with David by her charm and intelligence, became David's wife. What aspect of New Testament truth does this story foreshadow?

If Nabal stands for the Jewish nation which spurned their Lord and Saviour when graciously visited by Him, Abigail must foreshadow the believing remnant. Israel would have become like Sodom and Gomorrah had it not been for the believing remnant (Romans 9:29). Israel was spared only for the elect's sake, just as Nabal was spared a violent death only by the importunity of his discerning wife. But this state of affairs did not continue for long since the Jewish state was destroyed soon after by the Romans. The believing remnant, foreshadowed by Abigail, is destined to become the bride of the Lamb.

Nabal (meaning "Fool") lived in Maon ("Habitation", used of God's dwelling-place, the temple, 2 Chronicles 36:15; Psalm 26:8), and his possessions were in Carmel (meaning "gardenland"). He was blessed in every possible way. Like Israel he lived in a rich and fertile land. He was moreover visited and befriended by David himself, as Israel was by Christ. Nabal however was churlish and ungrateful. He spurned the kindness and protection which had been undeserved. He professed not to know whence his benefactor had come from, though his wife knew better. In all points Nabal is a type of churlish Israel, the rich fool of the parable (Luke 12:16-21).

We read also that Nabal was *shearing* his sheep (25:2, 4, 7, 11). It is always the careless, greedy shepherds (typologically speaking) who shear their sheep. Of this kind were Laban (Genesis 31:19), Judah (Genesis 38:12, 13), Absalom (2 Samuel 12:23, 24), and the murderers of Christ (Isaiah 53:7; Acts 8:32). Good shepherds like Abel (Genesis 4:2), Jacob (30:36), Joseph (37:2), Moses (Exodus 3:1), David (1 Samuel 16:11; 17:34), and the Lord (Psalm 23; 80:1; John 10) are represented as tending, keeping, feeding, and leading the flock, not as fleecing it for their own advantage. Nabal prefigures the type of shepherd condemned in Ezekiel 34:

> "Woe to the shepherds of Israel who only take care of themselves! Should not shepherds take care of the flock? You eat the curds clothe yourselves with the wool and slaughter the choice animals, but you do not take care of the flock …. This is what the sovereign Lord says: I am against the shepherds and will hold them accountable for my flock. I will remove them from tending the flock so that the shepherds can no longer feed themselves. I will rescue my flock from their mouths, and it will no longer be food for them." (See verses 1-16)

David's wives

David's wives (and fiancée) are suggestive of different sections of the Jewish people who heard and responded to the gospel message. The first was Saul's daughter Merab. She was promised to David, but when the time came for the marriage she was given to someone else (18:17-19). Merab corresponds to those who hear the message about the kingdom but do not understand it; then the evil one comes and snatches away what was sown in the heart (Matthew 13:19).

The next was Saul's daughter Michal. She professed a genuine love for David and was actually married to him (18:20-29), but later on she also was given to someone else (25:44). Michal corresponds to those who hear the word and at once receive it with joy, but since they have no root they only last for a short time. When trouble or persecution comes because of the word, they quickly fall away (Matthew 13:20, 21). She was given to Phalti ("Escaped"), son of Laish ("Lion") which was of Gallim ("Heaps"). One wonders what kind of husband he was!

From this liaison she was rescued by David (2 Samuel 3:14-16). But "when she saw King David leaping and dancing before the Lord, she despised him in her heart" (6:16). For her pride and hardness of heart "Michal daughter of Saul had no children to the day of her death" (6:23). Her trouble was that she remained too much a daughter of Saul and never became a devoted wife of David.

David's other two wives mentioned in 1 Samuel, Ahinoam and Abigail, correspond to those who hear the word and understand it, and produce a crop, yielding a hundred, sixty or thirty times what was sown (Matthew 13:23). They faithfully accompanied David during the time of his rejection and exile and shared in his suffering. They reflect the church of the Acts period which willingly accepted both suffering and exile for the sake of its rejected Lord.

David was forced to seek refuge among the Philistines in order to escape from Saul (1 Samuel 27) He took up residence with Achish king of Gath, taking with him Ahinoam and Abigail. In the same way the disciples were scattered abroad as a result of the persecution and the martyrdom of Stephen (Acts 8:1, 4; 11:19, 20). By this means the church became established in Gentile lands, while the unbelieving Jews back home were served by the apostles who remained behind.

Soon after, shortly before the death of Saul, David's city Ziklag was captured by the Amalekites (1 Samuel 30). The city was burnt to the ground and the entire population, including Ahinoam and Abigail, were taken captive. David in great distress inquired of the Lord what he should do. He was told that if he pursued the Amalekites he would over take them and every captured person would be rescued. He had 600 men with him, but 200 of them were too tired to go any further. These he left at Brook Besor ("Good Tidings"), while he and the remaining 400 pursued the Amalekites.

With the help of an Egyptian, left for dead in a field, David was able to track down the offending Amalekites. There they were, spread over a wide area, a huge company eating, drinking and reveling because of the great amount of spoil they had taken from Judah and the Philistines. David attacked them for a whole night and a day, killing nearly all of them, and rescuing everyone who had been captured, his two wives included. He then divided the spoil between those who had accompanied him and those who had been left behind, and sent gifts to each of the cities of Judah who had previously given him a welcome.

On one level we may see in this story Christ's triumph on the cross when He gave Himself up for His bride, the wife of the Lamb. "Having disarmed the powers and authorities, He made a public spectacle of them, triumphing over them by the cross" (Colossians 2:15). "When He ascended on high, He led captives in His train and gave gifts to men" (Ephesians 4:8)

On another level we may see in it an adumbration of future events. The Amalekites had invaded Judah, taking captive David's two wives. Thus will the forces of the Antichrist take captives of the Jewish people (the wife of the Lamb to be) when they overrun the land of Israel in the middle of the tribulation period. Believers for the most part will have already fled to the mountains in obedience to our Lord's warnings in Matthew 24:15, 16 (cp. Revelation 12:6). But the people as a whole will be completely taken by surprise. In view of their predicament the Lord Jesus, in His deep compassion for His captured people, will intervene on their behalf. With only a handful of faithful followers ("the clans of Judah", Zechariah 12:5) He will terrify the enemy hordes. "The feeblest among them will be like David, and the house of David will be like God, like the Angel of the Lord going before them" (12:8).

The enemy will be totally routed, the captured faithful delivered and the people prepared in heart and mind for the return of their Messiah and the establishment of His kingdom. All this might have taken place in the first century AD, but must now await the turn of events which will shift the focus of Divine activity back to the Jewish nation.

An important principle

On this occasion, after defeating the Amalekites, David laid down and enacted an important ordinance in Israel. It was that the share of the man who stayed with the supplies was to be the same as that of him who went down to the battle (30:24). In this situation the 200 men who had been too weary to proceed and had remained with the supplies at the Brook Besor had an equal share of the plunder as the 400 who had vanquished the Amalekites.

The purpose of the ordinance was to ensure that those who were unable to take part in the action, through no fault of their own, should not finally lose out or be held in dishonor. The same concern is shared by our Lord as may be seen or applied in various ways:

1) God gives great honour to those parts of the body that most lack it (1 Corinthians 12:24)

2) The eleventh hour workers are given the same wages as those who were hired first (Matthew 20:1-16)

3) In the great battle of Zechariah 12 the inhabitants of Jerusalem who fight the battle will not have mot glory than the other cities and towns of Judah. On the contrary, "The Lord will save the dwellings of Judah. First, so that the honour of the house of David and of Jerusalem's inhabitants my not be greater than that of Judah" (Zechariah 12:7).

4) Those who are still alive at the coming of the Lord will have no advantage over those who have fallen asleep. In fact the dead in Christ will rise first (1 Thessalonians 4:13-18). God will bring with Jesus those who have fallen asleep, whereas the living will be caught up with them in the clouds to meet the Lord in the air.

5) On the day that Christ rewards the faithful, it will not only be those who have been in the thick of the battle, such as missionaries and evangelists, who will be commended for their service, but also those who have stayed behind with prayer, the study of the Word and less conspicuous callings. "Christ is omnipotent and merciful. He rewards those who tarry in patience with the stuff, as well as those who go forth on the march, and fight valiantly in the battle" (Bishop Hall)

Saul's death

Saul, who had refused to repent, no longer had even David to prick his conscience. Abandoned by both David (the gospel of the kingdom) and Samuel (the word of prophecy, 25:1; 28:6) he quickly sunk into witchcraft and despair. Finally he died in Mount Gilboa. Saul's suicide points to the national suicide of that nation which judged itself unworthy of eternal life (Acts 13:46).

The first book of Samuel ends like some Shakespearean tragedy with the death of Saul and nearly all his family. "When the armour-bearer saw that Saul was dead, he too fell on his sword and died with him. So Saul and three of his sons and his armour-bearer and all his men died together the same day" (31:5-6). Almost the whole land of Israel was now in the possession of the Philistines, as Judea was in the possession of the Romans after the war of AD 66-70. With Saul died three of his sons, including Jonathan, signifying the end of that dispensation and the inauguration of a new age centred on Christ alone.

In the death of Saul and his sons we see foreshadowed the rejection of the Jewish nation at the end of the Acts period. In the fact that Jonathan died as well is the truth foreshadowed that even the Israel of God ceased to exist when the nation as a whole was abandoned. The nation became Lo-Ammi, Not God's people, but the believing remainder became God's people in an even fuller and more wonderful sense. They became members of a new Body, whose Head is none other than Christ Himself, whose residence is in the heavenly realms far above all rule and authority, whose election precedes the foundation of the world, and whose hope is to appear with Christ in glory. To that Body we Gentiles also belong, since in Christ we are all one body, every distinction between Jew and Gentile having been removed for the duration of this present period.

More on David

**David's son and The Son of David
By Michael Penny**

With a mixture of devotion and exposition, and with a blend of teaching and application, we are given some valuable insights and lessons gleaned from David's disastrous treatment of Bathsheba and her husband Uriah. It is, indeed, a case of God being able to turn all things to the good! Who would have thought that any good could have come from horrendous sins as adultery and murder?

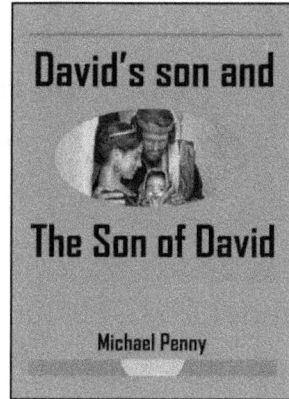

This book is also available as
eBooks from Amazon and Apple

And as KDP paperback from Amazon

About the Author

Charles Ozanne was born in Crowborough, Sussex, in 1936. He read Theology at Oxford before undertaking research in the book of Revelation for his PhD at the University of Manchester under F. F. Bruce. Some of his recent publications for the Open Bible Trust have a critique of Replacement Theology entitled *God's Plan for Israel: Replacement or Restoration?* And a work looking at *The Sabbath and Circumcision*. Both are available as eBooks.

His latest major works are *Empires of the End-Time* and *Understanding the New Testament*, available as perfect-bound paperbacks and as eBooks. For further details of all his writings, please visit:

www.obt.org.uk/charles-ozanne

Charles Ozanne is a regular contributor to *Search* magazine

For a free sample of
The Open Bible Trust's magazine Search,
please email

admin@obt.org.uk

or visit

www.obt.org.uk/search

Also by Charles Ozanne

The following is a selection.

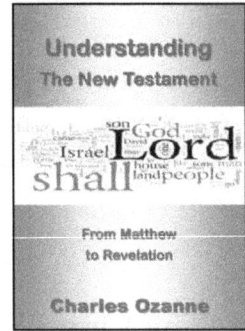

Israel's Appointed Feasts

Sensational Truth in Ephesians

Understanding The New Testament
From Matthew to Revelation

****

For more information on these please visit
www.obt.org.uk

They can be ordered from that website and from
The Open Bible Trust
Fordland Mount, Upper Basildon,
Reading, RG8 8LU, UK.

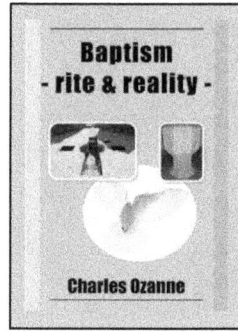

God's Plan for Israel:
Replacement or Restoration?

Empires of the End-Times
Through Daniel's Telescopic Lens

Baptism:
Rite and reality

****

**These books are also available as
eBooks from Amazon and Apple**

And as KDP paperback from Amazon

About this book

Samuel, Saul and David
(Types in 1 Samuel)

This excellent booklet deals with 'types' in 1 Samuel. It focuses on:

- Samuel, the priest,
- Saul, the first King, and
- David, a man after God's own heart.

In what ways are each of these three men a 'type' of Christ?

Publications of The Open Bible Trust must be in accordance with its evangelical, fundamental and dispensational basis. However, beyond this minimum, writers are free to express whatever beliefs they may have as their own understanding, provided that the aim in so doing is to further the object of The Open Bible Trust. A copy of the doctrinal basis is available at

www.obt.org.uk/doctrinal-basis

or from:

THE OPEN BIBLE TRUST
Fordland Mount, Upper Basildon,
Reading, RG8 8LU, UK.